THE MONSTER LOVES HIS LABYRINTH

THE MONSTER LOVES
HIS LABYRINTH

Notebooks

Charles Simic

AUSABLE PRESS
2008

Cover art: "Goodbye to All That," by Varujan Boghosian
2006. Paper collage, 9.75 x 7.25 inches
Collection of Kathryn & David Heleniak
Courtesy of Lori Bookstein Fine Art
Photo by Paul Waldman

Author portrait: Saul Steinberg, "Charles Simic, 1993"
Sketchbook page
Saul Steinberg Papers, Yale Collection of American Literature,
Beinecke Rare Book and Manuscript Collection, Yale University
© The Saul Steinberg Foundation/Artists Rights Society (ARS), New York

Design and composition by Ausable Press
The type is Menhart Pro.
Cover design by Rebecca Soderholm

Published by
Ausable Press
1026 Hurricane Road
Keene, NY 12942
www.ausablepress.org

Distributed to the trade by
Consortium Book Sales & Distribution
Perseus Distribution Services
1094 Flex Drive
Jackson, TN 38301-5070
Toll-free: (800) 283-3572
Fax: (800) 351-5073
Consortium Offices: (651) 221-9035

The acknowledgments appear on page 115 and constitute a
continuation of the copyright page.

Library of Congress Cataloging-in-Publication Data

Simic, Charles 1938—
The monster loves his labyrinth : notebooks/ by Charles Simic.—1st ed.
p. cm.
ISBN 978-1-931337-40-3 (pbk. : alk. paper)
I. Title.

PS3569.14725M66 2008
811'.54—dc22
2007049832

for Jonathan Aaron

I

Late night on MacDougal Street. An old fellow comes up to me and says: "Sir, I'm writing the book of my life and I need a dime to complete it." I give him a dollar.

Another night in Washington Square Park, a fat woman with fright wig says to me: "I'm Esther, the goddess of Love. If you don't give me a dollar, I'll put a curse on you." I give her a nickel.

One of those postwar memories: a baby carriage pushed by a humpbacked old woman, her son sitting in it, both legs amputated.

She was haggling with the greengrocer when the carriage got away from her. The street was steep so it rolled downhill with the cripple waving his crutch, his mother screaming for help, and everybody else laughing as if they were in the movies. Buster Keaton or somebody like that about to go over a cliff . . .

One laughed because one knew it would end well. One was surprised when it didn't.

I didn't tell you how I got lice wearing a German helmet. This used to be a famous story in our family. I remember those winter evenings just after the War with everybody huddled around the stove, talking and worrying late into the night. Sooner or later, it was inevitable, somebody would bring up my German helmet full of lice. They thought it was the funniest thing they ever heard. Old people had tears of laughter in their eyes. A kid dumb enough to walk around with a German helmet full of lice. They were crawling all over it. Any fool could see them!

I sat there saying nothing, pretending to be equally amused, nodding my head while thinking to myself, what a bunch of idiots! All of them! They had no idea how I got the helmet, and I wasn't about to tell them.

It was in those first days just after the liberation of Belgrade, I was up in the old cemetery with a few friends, kind of snooping around. Then, all of a sudden, we saw them! A couple of German soldiers, obviously dead, stretched out on the ground. We drew closer to take a better look. They had no weapons. Their boots were gone, but there was a helmet that had fallen to the side of one of them. I don't remember what the others got, but I went for the helmet. I tiptoed so as not to wake the dead man. I also kept my eyes averted. I never saw his face, even if sometimes I think I did. Everything else about that moment is still intensely clear to me.

That's the story of the helmet full of lice.

Beneath the swarm of high-flying planes we were eating watermelon. While we ate the bombs fell on Belgrade. We watched the smoke rise in the distance. We were hot in the garden and asked to take our shirts off. The watermelon made a ripe, cracking noise as my mother cut it with a big knife. We also heard what we thought was thunder, but when we looked up, the sky was cloudless and blue.

My mother heard a man plead for his life once. She remembers the stars, the dark shapes of trees along the road on which they were fleeing the Austrian army in a slow-moving ox-cart. "That man sounded terribly frightened out there in the woods," she says. The cart went on. No one said anything. Soon they could hear the river they were supposed to cross.

In my childhood women mended stockings in the evening. To have a "run" in one's stocking was cata-strophic. Stockings were expensive, and so was electricity.

We would all sit around the table with a single lamp, my grandmother reading the papers, we children pretending to do our homework, while watching my mother spreading her red-painted fingernails inside the transparent stocking.

In the biography of the Russian poet, Marina Tsvetaeva, I read that her first poetry reading in Paris took place on February 6, 1925, and the newspaper announcement says that there were also three musicians on the program, Madame Cunelli, who sang old Italian songs, Professor Mogilewski, who played violin, and V. E. Byutsov, who was on piano. This was astonishing! Madame Cunelli, whose first name was Nina, was a friend of my mother's. They both studied with the same voice teacher, Madame Kedrov, in Paris, and then somehow Nina Cunelli ended up in Belgrade during the Second World War where she taught me Russian and French children's songs, which I still know well. I remember that she was a beautiful woman, a little older than my mother, and that she went abroad after the War ended.

There was a maid in our house who let me put my hand under her skirt. I was five or six years old. I can still remember the dampness of her crotch and my surprise that there was all that hair there. I couldn't get enough of it. She would crawl under the table where I had my military fort and my toy soldiers. I don't remember what was said, if anything. Just her hand, firmly guiding mine to that spot.

They sit on the table, the tailors do. At least, they used to. A street of dim shops in Belgrade where we went to have my father's coat narrowed and shortened so it would fit me. The tailor got off the table and stuck pins in my shoulder. "Don't squirm," my mother said. Outside it was getting dark. Large snowflakes fell.

Years later in New York, on the same kind of afternoon, a dry-cleaning store window with an ugly, thick-legged woman on the chair in a white dress. She's having the hem raised by a gray-headed Jewish tailor, who kneels before her as if he is proposing marriage.

There was an expensive-looking suitcase on the railroad tracks, and they were afraid to come near it. Far from any station, on a stretch of track bordered by orchards where they had been stealing plums that afternoon. The suitcase, she remembers, had colorful labels, of what were probably world-famous hotels and ocean liners. During the War, of course, one heard of bombs, special ones, in the shape of toys, pens, soccer balls, exotic birds—so why not suitcases? For that reason they left it where it was.

"I always wondered what was in it," my wife says. We were talking about the summer of 1944, of which we both had only a few clear recollections.

The world was going up in flames and I was studying violin. The baby Nero sawing away . . .

My teacher's apartment was always cold. A large, almost empty room with a high ceiling already in shadow. I remember the first few screechy notes my violin would make and my teacher's stern words of reprimand. I was terrified of that old woman. I also loved her because after the scolding she would give me something to eat. Something rare and exotic, like chocolate filled with sweet liqueur. We'd sit in that big empty room, almost dark now. I'd be eating and she'd be watching me eat.

"Poor child," she'd say, and I thought it had to do with my not practicing enough, my being dim-witted when she tried to explain something to me, but today I'm not sure that's what she meant. In fact, I suspect she had something else entirely in mind. That's why I am writing this, to find out what it was.

When my grandfather was dying from diabetes, when he had already had one leg cut off at the knee and they were threatening to do the same to the other, his old buddy, Savo Lozanic, used to visit him every morning to keep him company. They would reminisce about this and that and even have a few laughs.

One morning my grandmother had to leave him alone in the house, as she had to attend the funeral of a distant relative. That's what gave him the idea. He hopped out of bed and into the kitchen, where he found candles and matches. He got back into his bed, somehow placed one candle above his head and the other at his feet, and lit them. Finally he pulled the sheet over his face and began to wait.

When his friend knocked, there was no answer. The door being unlocked, he went in, calling from time to time. The kitchen was empty. A fat gray cat slept on the dining room table. When he entered the bedroom and saw the bed with the sheet and lit candles, he let out a wail and then broke into sobs as he groped for a chair to sit down.

"Shut up, Savo," my grandfather said sternly from under his sheet. "Can't you see I'm only practicing?"

I leave the dentist's chair after what seems an eternity. It's an evening in June. I'm walking the tree-lined streets full of dark, whispering trees in my neighborhood in Belgrade. The streets are poorly lit, but there are people about strolling close to each other as if they were lovers. The thought crosses my mind that this is the happiest moment in my life.

In Chicago, in the 1950's, there was still an old woman with a street organ and a monkey. She turned the crank with both hands while the monkey went around with a tin cup. It was some vaguely familiar tune that made our grandmothers sigh in their youth.

The woman looked like she must've known the cow that started the Great Fire. Later she married an Italian with a street organ. At times he kissed her with the monkey still on his shoulder.

The animal I saw looked young and full of mischief. He wore a tattered coat with brass buttons, which he must have inherited from his father. That day they had for an audience a small boy who wanted one of the monkey's bells. His beautiful mother kept pulling his arm to go, but he wouldn't budge. The old woman turning the crank had her eyes raised to heaven in a manner favored by saints who are being tempted by demons.

Another story about time. This one about the time it took them to quit their cells after beginning to suspect that the Germans were gone. In that huge prison in Milan all of a sudden you could hear a pin drop. Eventually they thought it best to remove their shoes before walking out.

My father was still tiptoeing hours later crossing a large empty piazza. There was a full moon above the dark palaces. His heart was in his mouth.

"It was just like an opera stage," he says. "All

lit up, but nobody in the audience, and nobody in the orchestra pit. Nevertheless, I felt like singing. Or perhaps screaming?"

He did neither. The year was 1944.

The streets are empty, it's raining, and we are sitting in the Hotel Sherman bar listening to the bluesy piano. I'm not yet old enough to order a drink, but my father's presence is so authoritative and intimidating that when he orders for me the waiters never dare to ask about my age.

We talk. My father remembers a fly that wouldn't let him sleep one summer afternoon fifty years ago. I tell him about an old gray overcoat twice my size, which my mother made me wear after the War. It was wintertime. People on the street would sometimes stop and watch me. The overcoat trailed the ground and made walking difficult. One day I was standing on the corner waiting to cross when a young woman gave me a small coin and walked away. I was so embarrassed.

"Was she pretty?" my father asks.

"Not at all," I tell him. "She looked like a hick, maybe a nun."

"A Serbian Ophelia," my father thinks.

It's possible. Anything is possible.

The huge crowd cheering the dictator; the smiling faces of children offering flowers in welcome. How many times have I seen that? And always the same blonde little girl curtsying! Here she is surrounded by the high boots of the dignitaries and a couple of tightly leashed police dogs. The monster himself is patting her on the head and whispering in her ear.

I look in vain for someone with a troubled face.

The exiled general's grandson was playing war with his cheeks puffed to imitate bombs exploding. The grim daughter wrote down the old man's reminiscences. The whole apartment smelled of bad cooking. The general was in a wheelchair. He wore a bib and smoked a cigar. The daughter smiled for me and my mother in a way that made her sharp little teeth show.

I liked the general better. He remembered some prime minister pretending to wipe his ass with a treaty he had just signed, the captured enemy officers drinking heavily and toasting some cabaret singer from their youth.

It's your birthday. The child you were appears on the street wearing a stupid grin. He wants to take you by the hand, but you won't let him.

"You've forgotten something," he whispers. And you, quiet as a mutt around an undertaker, since, of course, he (the child) doesn't exist.

There was an old fellow at the *Sun Times*, who was boss when I first came and worked as a mail clerk, who claimed to have read everything. His father was a janitor at the university library in Urbana, and Stanley, for that was his name, started as a kid. At first I didn't believe any of it; then I asked him about Gide, whom I was then reading. He recited for me the names of the major novels and their plots. What about Isaac Babel, Alain Fournier, Aldous Huxley, Ford Madox Ford? The same thing. It was amazing! Everything I had read or heard of he had already read. "You should be on a quiz show, Stanley," people who overheard us said. Stanley had never been to college and had worked for the papers most of his life.

He had a stutter, so I guess that explains why he never married or got ahead. So, all he did was read books. I had the impression that he loved every book he read. Only superlatives for Stanley, one book better than the other. If I started to criticize, he'd get pissed off. Who do I think I am? Smartass, he called me, and wouldn't talk to me about books for a few days. Stanley was pure enthusiasm. I was giddy myself at the thought of another book waiting for me to read at home.

In Chicago there was a tremendous suspicion of the Eastern literary establishment. The working people never get portrayed in their books, I heard people say all the time. Most of the people I met were leftist intellectuals from working-class and immigrant backgrounds. These were Jews, Poles, Germans, Irish. They had relatives who worked in factories. They knew America could be a cruel place, an unjust country. After I saw South Chicago and Gary, Indiana, I had to admit they had a point. Both places, with their steel mills in smoke and fire, were like hell out of Hieronymus Bosch. The ugliness and poverty of industrial Chicago was an enormous influence on me. It prevented me from forgetting where I came from. A big temptation for all immigrants with intellectual pretensions is to outdo the natives in their love of Henry James and whatever he represents. You want to blend in, so you're always looking for the role models. It's very understandable. Who wants to look and talk like a foreigner forever!

The night of my farewell dinner in Chicago, I got very drunk. At some point, I went to the bathroom and could not find my way back. The restaurant was large and full of mirrors. I would see my friends seated in the distance, but when I hurried toward them, I would come face to face with myself in a mirror. With my new beard I did not recognize myself immediately and almost apologized. In the end, I gave up and sat at an old man's table. He ate in silence and I lit a cigarette. Time passed. The place was emptying. The old man finally wiped his mouth and pushed his full, untouched wine glass toward me. I would have stayed with him indefinitely if one of the women from our party hadn't found me and led me outside.

Did I lie a little? Of course. I gave the impression that I had lived for years on the Left Bank and often sat at the tables of the famous cafés watching the existentialists in their passionate arguments. What justified these exaggerations in my eyes was the real possibility that I could have done something like that. Everything about my life already seemed a fluke, a series of improbable turns of events, so in my case fiction was no stranger than truth. Like when I told the woman on the train from Chicago that I was a Russian. I described our apartment in Leningrad, the terrors of the long siege during the War, the deaths of my parents before a German firing squad which we children had to witness, the DP camps in Europe. At some point during the long night I had to go to the bathroom and simply laugh.

How much of it did she believe? Who knows? In the morning she gave me a long kiss in parting, which could have meant anything.

My father and his best friend talking about how some people resemble animals. The birdlike wife of so and so, for example. The many breeds of dogs and their human look-alikes. The lady who is a cow. The widow next door who is a tigress, etc.

"And what about me?" says my father's friend.

"You look like a rat, Tony," he replies without a moment's hesitation, after which they just sit drinking without saying another word.

"You look like a young Franz Schubert," the intense-looking woman told me as we were introduced.

At that same party, I spoke to a lawyer who insisted we had met in London two years before. I explained my accent to a doctor by telling him that I was raised by a family of deaf-mutes.

There was a girl there, too, who kept smiling sweetly at me without saying anything. Her mother told me that I reminded her of her brother, who was executed by the Germans in Norway. She was going to give me more details, but I excused myself, telling everyone that I had a sudden and terrible toothache that required immediate attention.

I got the idea of sleeping on the roof in Manhattan on hot nights from my mother and father. That's what they did during the War, except it wasn't a roof but a large terrace on the top floor of a building in downtown Belgrade. There was a blackout, of course. I remember immense starry skies, and how silent the city was. I would begin to speak, but someone—I could not tell for a moment who it was—would put a hand over my mouth.

Like a ship at sea we were with stars and clouds up above. We were sailing full speed ahead. "That's where the infinite begins," I remember my father pointing with his long, dark hand.

If my father has a ghost, he's standing outside some elegant men's store on Madison Avenue on a late summer evening. A tall man studying a pair of brown suede Italian shoes. He himself is impeccably dressed in a tan suit, a blue shirt of an almost purple hue with a silk tie the color of rusty rose. He seems in no hurry. At the age of fifty-three, with his hair thinning and slicked back, he could be an Italian or a South American. Belle Georgio, one waitress in Chicago used to call him. No one would guess by his appearance that he is almost always broke.

I'm packing parcels in the Lord & Taylor basement during the Christmas rush with a bunch of losers. One fellow is an inventor. He has a new kind of aquarium with piped music, which makes it look as if the fish are doing water ballet, but the world is not interested. Another man supports three ex-wives, so he has a night job in addition to this one. His eyes close all the time. He's so pale, he could pass for a stiff in an open coffin.

Then there's Felix, a mousy fellow a bit older than I who claims to be a distant relative of the English royal family. One time he brought the chart of his family tree to make us stop laughing and explained the connection. What did not make sense was his poverty. He said he was a writer but wouldn't tell us what kind. "Are you writing porno?" one Puerto Rican girl asked him.

Her name was Rosie. She liked boxing. One time she and I went on a date to watch the fights at the Garden. We sat in the Spanish section. "Kill him! Kill him!" she screamed all evening without interruption. At the end she was so tired she wouldn't even have a drink with me, and had to rush home.

At a poetry reading given by Allen Tate I met a young poet who was attending a workshop given by Louise Bogan at NYU. I sat in a few times and accompanied my new friends for beers after class. One day I even showed two of my poems to Bogan. One was called "Red Armchair," and it had to do with an old chair thrown out on the sidewalk for the trashmen to pick up. The other poem I don't remember. Bogan was very kind. She fixed a few things but was generally encouraging, which surprised me, since I didn't think much of the poems myself.

The other critique of my poetry came later that fall and it was devastating. I had met a painter in a bar, an older fellow living in poverty with a wife and two small kids in a cold water flat in the Village, where he painted huge, realistic canvases of derelicts in the manner of 1930's social realism. A skyscraper and underneath a poor man begging. The message was obvious, but the colors were nice.

Despite the difference in our ages, we saw each other quite a bit, talking art and literature, until one day I showed him my poems. We were sitting in his kitchen with a bottle of whiskey between us. He leaned back in the chair and read the poems slowly, slowly while I watched him closely. At some point I began to detect annoyance in him and then anger. Finally, he looked at me as if seeing me for the first time and said something like: "Simic, I thought you were a smart kid. This is pure shit you're writing!"

I was prepared for gentle criticism in the manner of Louise Bogan, even welcomed it, but his bluntness stunned me. I left in a daze. I was convinced he was right. If I'd had a pistol, I would have shot myself on the spot. Then, little by little, mulling over what he had said, I got pissed off. There were some good things in my poems, I thought. "Fuck him," I shouted to some guy who came my way in the street. Of course, he was right, too, and it hurt me that he was, but all the same.

I came out of my daze just as I was entering Central Park on 59th Street. I had walked more than sixty blocks totally oblivious of my surroundings. I sat on a bench and reread my poems, crossing out most of the lines, attempting to rewrite them then and there, still angry, still miserable, and at the same time grimly determined.

There was this old guy in Washington Square Park who used to lecture me about Sacco and Vanzetti and the great injustice done to them. We'd share a bench from time to time, and I'd hear him say again and again how if shit was worth money the poor would be born without assholes. He wore gray gloves, walked with a cane, tipped his hat to ladies, and worried about me. "A kid just off the boat," he'd say to someone passing by. "Sure to get screwed if he doesn't watch out."

I went to see Ionesco's *Bald Soprano* with Boris. It was being presented at a small theater in the Village. There were only six people in the audience, and that included the two of us. They gave the performance anyway. When it came to the love scene with the woman who has three noses, the actors got carried away on the couch. Their voices went down to a whisper as they started undressing each other. Boris and I just looked at each other. The other four people had suddenly become invisible. Well, they didn't fuck each other, but they came very close. I have no recollection of the rest of the play except that at the exit the streets were covered with newly fallen snow.

I was five minutes late from lunch at the insurance company where I was working and my boss chewed me out for being irresponsible in front of twenty or thirty other drudges. I sat at my desk for a while fuming, then I rose slowly, wrapped my scarf around my neck and put my gloves on in plain view of everybody, and walked out without looking back. I didn't have an overcoat and on the street it was snowing, but I felt giddy, deliriously happy at being free.

"My boy seeks the secret and the meaning of Time," we are told upon entering. If we weren't told, we'd say he's just staring out of the window at the rain. His mother wants us to be very quiet as we inspect the room she's thinking of renting.

     "Povera e nuda via, Filosofia," wrote the Italian poet Petrarch. The rain getting heavier and then the sound of thunder over Manhattan.

The face of my daughter lit by a table lamp while she sucks a finger pricked by a compass. A drop of blood already fallen on the black letters and numerals of the difficult homework, as she worries whether to hand it in, just as it is, to the stern old nun who'll make her stand in front of the class waiting for the verdict . . . The spring day bright with sunlight. The nun's small, tight fist clouding the answer.

We were on our third bottle of wine when he said he was going to show me the pictures of his girlfriend. To my surprise, the photographs spread out on the table were of a naked woman shamelessly displaying herself. Leaning over my shoulder he wanted me to note each detail, her crotch, her ass, her breasts, until I felt aroused. It was an odd situation. My host's pregnant wife was asleep in the next room. The photographs were spread all over the dining room table. There must've been close to a hundred of them. I looked and I listened. From time to time, I could hear the wife snore.

Approaching Manhattan on the train at night, I remember the old Polish and Ukrainian women wielding their mops in the brightly lit towers. I'd be working on some ledger that wouldn't balance, and they'd be scrubbing floors on their knees. They were fat and they all wore flowered dresses. The youngest would stand on a chair and dust off the portrait of the grim founder of the company. The old black man who ran the elevator would bow to them like a headwaiter in a fancy restaurant as he took them from one floor to the next. That would make them laugh. You'd see they had teeth missing. More than a few teeth missing.

It was a window with a view of a large office with many identical desks at which men and women sat working. A woman got up with papers in hand and walked the length of the floor to where a man rose to meet her at the other end. He waved his arms as he talked, while she stood before him with her head lowered, and I went on tying my necktie in the hotel room across the street. I was about to turn away from the window when I realized that the man was yelling at the woman, and that she was sobbing.

Here's a scene for you. My father and I are walking down Madison, when I spot a blue overcoat in a store called the British American House. We study it, comment on the cut, and my father suggests I try it on. I know he has no money, but he insists since it's beginning to snow a little and I'm only wearing a tweed jacket. We go in, I put it on, and it fits perfectly. Immediately, I'm in love with it. We ask the price and it's two hundred dollars—which was a lot of money in 1959. Too bad, I think, but then my father asks me if I want it. I think maybe he's showing off in front of the salesman or he's come into some money he hasn't told me about. "Do you want it?" he asks again while the salesman goes to attend to another customer. "You've no money, George," I remind him, expecting him to contradict me or come to his senses. "Don't worry," is his reply.

I've seen him do this before and it embarrasses me. He asks for the boss and the two of them sequester themselves for a while, while I stand around waiting for us to be kicked out. Instead, he emerges triumphant and I wear the overcoat into the street. A born con man. His manner and appearance inspired such confidence that with a small down payment and promise to pay the rest in a week or two, he'd get what he wanted. This was in the days before credit cards and credit bureaus when store owners had to make such decisions on the spot. They trusted him, and he did pay eventually whatever he owed. The crazy thing was that he pulled this stunt only in the best stores. It would never occur to him to ask for credit from a grocer, and yet he often went hungry despite his huge salary.

My father had phenomenal debts. He borrowed money any chance he had and paid his bills only when absolutely necessary. It was nothing for him to spend the rent money the night before it was due. I lived in terror of my landlords and landladies while he seemingly never worried. We'd meet after work and he'd suggest dinner in a French restaurant and I'd resist, knowing it was his rent money he was proposing to spend. He'd describe the dishes and wines we could have in tantalizing detail, and I'd keep reminding him of the rent. He'd explain to me slowly, painstakingly, as if I were feeble-minded, that one should never worry about the future. "We'll never be so young as we are tonight," he'd say. "If we are smart, tomorrow we'll figure out how to pay the rent." In the end, who could say no? I never did.

On the street corner the card trickster was shuffling his three cards using a large cardboard box as a table. The cards, the quick hands fluttered. It looked like a cock fight. Five of us watching without expression, our heads, in the meantime, buzzing with calculations and visions of riches. The day was cold so we all had to squint.

"Tough guys," he said, "time to place your bets."

I became more and more lucid the later it got. This was always my curse. Everybody was already asleep. I tried to wake my dearest, but she drew me down on her breasts sleepily. We made love, slowly, languidly, and then I talked to her for hours about the necessity of poetry while she slept soundly.

II

Once again, I find myself on the North Pole. I have no sled, no dogs and I'm dressed for bed. You ask me if I'm cold? Of course I'm cold, you idiots.

Dark December evening. In the church the saints are awake watching the snow fall.

Ariadne plays the piano one finger at a time like a funeral in the rain. Theseus wants something we can all dance to. The Minotaur whom everybody here calls dumbbell nods his head happily.

The child beaters took their little son to church on Sundays.

Sleepwalkers unite. Congregate on the rooftops at midnight.

I traveled over some bad roads in my childhood. It's no wonder I have a few loose screws.

History is a cookbook. The tyrants are chefs. The philosophers write menus. The priests are waiters. The military men are bouncers. The singing you hear is the poets washing dishes in the kitchen.

The kindness of one human being to another in times of mass hatred and violence deserves more respect than the preaching of all the churches since the beginning of time.

Headlines in supermarket tabloids:

A FLY TERRORIZES KANSAS.
CANNIBAL WAITER EATS SIX DINERS IN L.A.
BABY SMUGGLED INSIDE A WATERMELON.

Stupidity is the secret spice historians have difficulty identifying in this soup we keep slurping.

The number of watches and clocks to be found today must be an affront to eternity.

Let us not forget that Romeo and Juliet, too, used to fart and scratch their asses from time to time.

I remember a small boy saying in the lull between two waves of planes during a bombing raid: "I want to go pipi, Mama."

I lay in the dark thinking about the vastness of the universe while my wife snored away on the next pillow.

Here's a fifty-year-old wine of noble vintage ready to be poured down the drain.

An old man singing "Oh Marie" at the top of his lungs while being shoved handcuffed toward a police car with its lights flashing.

Oh, to be inside a mailbox next to a letter declaring love and steamy kisses to an unknown recipient.

Faces in the crowd. They were going about their business when they saw me staring at them and they were either amused or they turned away annoyed. All the time they were hiding in plain view and I found them out.

Riding on a sow, holding on to its ears and shouting, "Out of my way, chickens!" Did I really do that?

I'm a member of that minority which refuses to be part of any officially designated minority.

I like to hear a happy tune played sadly.

Sgt. Eric Schrump of the 5th Marine Regiment. "We had a great day. We killed a lot of people."

"The same crooks . . . wherever you go . . . regardless of regime, philosophy, creed, or color . . ." (Celine). That has been my experience too.

The Golden Age of American Literature. When cowboys used to read Emily Dickinson in the saddle, and the cops walking the beat carried a volume of Wallace Stevens in the pocket of their overcoats.

Every defense of poetry is a defense of folly.

The occupiers everywhere, I note, are outraged by the bad manners of the occupied who do nothing but complain about being mistreated.

The farther the injustice, the louder the outrage.

Sat up like a firecracker in bed, startled by the thought of my death.

Photographs show us what we do not have words to say.

Jazz is about happiness. Old happiness made into new happiness.

Religion: Turning the mystery of Being into a figure who resembles our grandfather sitting on the potty.

Snow arriving this morning at my door like a mail-order bride.

Sultry demoiselle Isabelle, smutty photo a succubus dangles before a monk kneeling in prayer.

Canned laughter on TV like beer cans tied to a car driving in the dark with no headlights.

The comedy of clocks: The clock the universe keeps and the one the roach running up my kitchen wall has just consulted.

Who said, "If God didn't want us to drink, why did he make wine so good?"

The Egyptian bronze mirror (1500 BC) in the British Museum where I managed to catch a blurred reflection of myself one rainy afternoon in 1982 is still there.

The new American Dream is to get to be very rich and still be regarded as a victim.

It's a kind of neighborhood where a rat is likely to keep a child as a pet.

Every nation is scared of the truth of what they have done to others.

Our rich are better at thieving than our thieves of common variety.

The chief role of a free press in democracy is to conceal that the country is ruled by a few.

Caterpillar, run over by a little girl's bike, twisting in pain.

While he sat thinking, he kept scratching his bald head with a match as if trying to set it on fire.

In Charon's boat I intend to give my seat to the first lady that comes along.

"This museum is full of forgeries," I whispered to her as I felt her ass. "I don't care," she replied a she put her hand on my crotch. "They look good to me."

The soul is a shadow cast by the light of consciousness. In the meantime, I can feel a sneeze coming.

True Tales of the Supernatural. How I ate twelve hot dogs at a ball game while my team kept losing.

Did solitary strollers whistle past graveyards in Cotton Mather's time, or were they as silent as the graves?

Short poem: Be brief and tell us everything.

Utopia: A rich chocolate cake protected from flies by a glass bell.

Slaughterhouse workers on their lunch hour sporting their bloody aprons.

When the children are asleep, the mice nibble the golden crumbs that have fallen on their covers.

Time, the voiceless, needs your big mouth tonight.

He took tipsy conventioneers to a funeral home with a promise that they'd see a live sex show and left them waiting among the coffins.

It happens that a cricket enters an abandoned house at the end of a road rarely traveled to sing as the night is falling.

An old man huddled over a urinal with a doomsday sign on his back.

He described his miserable life to a small white dog who sat with perked ears, wagging his little tail from time to time.

The waiter's name was Bartleby—or it should have been. He brought me two pieces of burnt toast on a cracked plate.

They led the small boy by the hand down the long row of brand new coffins.

I remember my father saying, "Let's have another bottle of wine so that when we rise from the table we can feel the earth turning under our feet."

Missing Cats Found by a Professional Medium, the card pinned on a bulletin board said. There was a phone number and the name Adele.

More tabloid news:

SHAKESPEARE'S DOG ATE HIS BEST, NEVER-
PERFORMED PLAY.

THE BONES OF ADAM AND EVE HAVE BEEN
FOUND IN THE ACT OF EMBRACING.

A MAN CHANGED HIMSELF THROUGH AN
OPERATION BACK INTO AN APE.

HELL IS SO OVERCROWDED, THE NEW ARRI-
VALS ARE BEING SENT TO HEAVEN.

Another sleepless night. I could hear the faucet drip in
the city morgue.

Little girl feeding pigeons breadcrumbs in the park and
cautioning them not to be so greedy.

A quartet playing free jazz in a club with a drunk
customer shouting, "How about a polka next?"

"This is the kind of place," my wife says, "where you
want the waiters to sit down with you and talk."

In the cards, Irene, I see a wedding dress for you, a
shoebox full of money and some murky goings-on with a
bow-legged man in a fish-house on a frozen lake.

The role of every patriotic journalist is to justify the
crimes our president and his administration have
committed.

We are the envy of the world. Our devils all go to church on Sunday.

The crows like one bare tree in my yard more than any other bare tree. Even the kids throwing rocks at them can't make them change their minds and lose their cool.

He prayed to God who couldn't wait for him to die so he can roast him over a slow fire.

"You can not shoe a flea," Russians say. Whoever coined the proverb forgot about poets.

At the tanning salon on Route 9, Regina, the Pizza Hut girl, lies naked with shades on.

The sunset sits down to a feast over the rooftops as the homeless make their beds in the streets.

The poet sees what the philosopher thinks.

Creaky old bedsprings, one-man blues-band.

The old Jew took me in the back of his store and showed me a drawer full of stained, old watch faces.

Death passing my door, jingling his passkeys.

An angel pinned in a box of dead butterflies.

This morning opening the papers I caught a whiff of evils to come.

A carpet worn out by the pacings of a local Hamlet selling cheaply at a yard sale.

In my grandmother's time all one needed was a broom to get to see the world and give the geese a chase in the sky.

A life of vice starts in the cradle. He loved crawling under the skirts of his big sister's friends. One of them let him stay there till he was an old man.

To lovers even their first names are poetry.

Softly now, the fleas are awake.

Today my shoes were shined by a hunchback who survived one of Stalin's labor camps.

A sign in Alabama. Love Power Church. Music and Miracles.

The servants of the rich and powerful are convinced that the rest of us envy them their servitude.

I'm the child of the rainy Sundays of my youth.

Like a cat, the heart sees far in the dark.

The magician folded the sheet of paper with my question over and over until no trace of it was left in his hand.

In an office of a business on the verge of bankruptcy, three mummified beings surrounded by antiquated adding machines and filing cabinets, their backs and graying heads bent obediently as if waiting for a reprimand from a superior who is about to arrive. Even the light falling on them is dusty.

A plague of clocks in cities where chance rules.

I knew a woman who collected black buttons she found in the street. Some years there'd be only one or two. When I asked her what for and why only black buttons, she shrugged her shoulders. She kept them in a jar on the coffee table. They seduced the eye. One button even had some thread left as if it had been torn in a hurry. A violent scene took place, a burst of passion on some dark doorway, and then she came along the next day and found the button.

Did anybody hear me sing today?

Nothing to do tonight but listen to hair grow on my head.

A window with a candlelit table. A couple in love left in a hurry for one of the dark bedrooms without first bothering to clear the plates.

The fresco of a young Sybil on a ceiling of a monastery in Florence. She appears frightened by what she knows.

"God has a plan for America," the preacher on TV said just as you came to bed carrying a bowl of cherries against your naked breasts.

A lone cloud stumbling across the sky like a beery accordionist in a German tavern.

There's a fortune to be made in America manufacturing cages for human beings.

The roadside stand
Was the place to be.
With you in a ditch
Squatting down to pee
And your skirt hiked
Way above your knee.

My old mother, exchanging whispers at dawn with a saint shot full of arrows.

The imagination has moments when it knows what the word "infinity" means.

A narrow street with windows weakly lit at dinner time and self-absorbed men and women standing around and an occasional child who eats alone looking at nothing.

Old woman stammering excuses to the pigeons for frightening them.

I made a paper plane out of my sadness. It flew around your lovely head and fell into your bowl of pea soup.

We are all stowaways on a ship of fools.

Ease your troubled spirit on a park bench, dear Sir. Exchange the phantoms of worldly success for the eyes of an adoring mutt.

Venus catches a cold without wine. Her nose is red and she has sniffles. "Drink up, drink up," I tell her, "and have some rat cheese."

33

He told me of a toy shop owned by an undertaker.

I saw a priest walk past a homeless woman sprawled on the sidewalk and look away. I regret not running after him and giving him a kick in the ass.

All my life I strove to make a small truth out of an infinity of errors.

Phone sex with Persephone in Hell, the ad said.

My conscience: A girl in white communion dress slumped over on a flophouse bed.

A waiter with a white napkin over his eyes. He starts toward our table with two bowls of soup and loses his way until he crashes into a wall. We are stunned, outraged and about to leave when another waiter with a white napkin over his eyes emerges from the kitchen carrying our steaks.

As far as I can tell, the universe has no visible means of support.

In the zoo I came across many animals as bored with life as I was.

One of the older of the gravediggers wore a black overcoat with a fur collar that may have once belonged to a judge or a bank president.

Four poets reading. "My pain is greater than yours," they kept shouting all night.

As a child, I saw faces on walls, ceilings, doorknobs and spoons. Then, one day, they were all gone.

The couple next door couldn't stop laughing all night. What's so funny? I wanted to shout through the wall, but was afraid they'd fall silent and leave me alone with my thoughts.

The beauty of a fleeting moment is eternal.

At the Inferno Amusement Park, the Tunnel of Love is under new management.

Birds sing to remind us that we have a soul.

Children running after a ball over a mass grave keep running.

They give me coffee,
They give me tea,
They give me everything
But the jailhouse key.

In a house closed up since last summer, the phone won't stop ringing.

Thatched myself over with words in the dark. Night after night, thatched myself anew against the infinite.

Millions were out to kill me. They fired cannons, dropped bombs, set villages on fire and shot my dog in the street. It's that mutt I still miss.

A tree full of dark leaves eager to tell us its dreams.

Free the guppies.

Night of the Hunter is being shown followed by *A Night at the Opera* and *The Night of the Living Dead*.

I bark back at the dog and he wags his tail at me.

In the park the grass was matted where two unknown lovers lay.

In that wedding cake grand hotel she had her purse stolen.

The madman with shaved head and intense glare who looked like the Russian poet Mayakovsky. He walked the avenue screaming at the top of his voice.

I'm willing to relocate to a rock in the sea.

Gravedigger, the truth is dark under your fingernails.

I'm everywhere and nowhere. A passenger on a ghost ship.

Cassiopeia and her retinue in full view over the astrologer's house.

I heard of a mind reader who could read what a lit match feared as it entered a dark house.

Torturers with happy faces, you made a prisoner strip naked and stand strung with electric wires like a Christmas tree while we sat sipping beer, one eye on the TV set, the other on the bartender who refills our glasses.

Black cat in the snow outside the house of the dead.

How to Make Bad Wine Good. 1000 recipes. Send $19.95 to Box 192, Fool's Paradise, NH.

I dreamt that God asked me for a blurb for his creation.

III

—They're not really object poems.
—What are they then?
—They are premonitions.
—About what?
—About the absolute otherness of the object.
—So, it's the absolute you've been thinking of?
—Of course.

Form is the visible side of content. The way in which the content becomes manifest. Form: Time turning into space and space turning into time simultaneously.

I admire Claude Levi Strauss's observation that all art is essentially reduction and Gertrude Stein's saying that poetry is vocabulary.

Chance as a tool with which to break up one's habitual associations. Once they're broken, use one of the pieces to launch yourself into the unknown.

We name one thing and then another. That's how time enters poetry. Space, on the other hand, comes into being through the attention we pay to each word. The more intense our attention, the more space, and there's a lot of space inside words.

Connotations have their non-Euclidean geometries.

A song sung while understanding each word—the way Billie Holiday or Bessie Smith did it.

Vitrac called chance a "lyric force." He's absolutely right. There's a kind of dreamy exhilaration in not knowing where one is going.

Seeing with eyes open and seeing with eyes closed. That's what Elizabeth Bishop's poem "The Fish" is about.

For imagination, inside every object there's another object hidden. The object inside is completely unlike the outside object, or the object inside is identical to the outside object, only more perfect. It all depends on one's metaphysics, or rather, whether one leans toward imagination or reason. The truth probably is that the outside and the inside are both identical and different.

My complaint about Surrealism: It worships imagination through the intellect.

Form thinks, not the content.
What the hell does that mean?
But, if form is time and time thinks . . .

The poem I want to write is impossible. A stone that floats.

Duncan's profound words: "The mysteries of here and there, above and below, now and then, demand new figures of me."

Avant-gardism: Seeing the history of art and literature as "progressing," the future being superior to the past, etc. For literary conservatives it's the other way around. There was once a Golden Age, and so on. We are just dwarfs on the back of giants, etc., etc.

Some twentieth-century intellectual types: Those who welcome the philosophical contradictions, those who ignore them, and those who despair because of them.

Form is not a "shape" but an "image," the way in which my inwardness seeks visibility.

Artaud: "No image satisfies me unless it is at the same time knowledge."

My ambition is to corner the reader and make him or her imagine and think differently.

The time of the poem is the time of expectation. I believe some Russian Formalist said something like that.

I'd like to show readers that the most familiar things that surround them are unintelligible.

There is a weather report in almost every folk poem. The sun is shining; it was snowing; the wind was blowing. . . . The folk poet knows that it's wise to immediately establish the connection between the personal and the cosmic.

Poetry is a way of knowledge, but most poetry tells us what we already know.

Between the truth that is heard and the truth that is seen, I prefer the silent truth of the seen.

If I make everything at the same time a joke and a serious matter, it's because I honor the eternal conflict between life and art, the absolute and the relative, the brain and the belly, etc. . . . No philosophy is good enough to overcome a toothache . . . that sort of thing.

Thought in art is customarily confused with didacticism, with paraphrasable content, with "message." Thought in genuine art is always none of these things.

Contradictory pulls when it comes to making a poem: to leave things as they are or to reimagine them; to represent or to reenact; to submit or to assert; artifice or nature, and so on. Like the cow the poet should have more than one stomach.

There are three kinds of poets: Those who write without thinking, those who think while writing, and those who think before writing.

Awe (as in Dickinson) is the beginning of metaphysics. The awe at the multiplicity of things and awe at their suspected unity.

To make something that doesn't yet exist, but which after its creation would look as if it had always existed.

The never-suspected, the always-awaited, the immediately-recognized new poem. It's like Christ's Second Coming.

The poet is a tea leaf reader of his own metaphors: I see a dark stranger, a voyage, a reversal of fortune, etc. You might as well get a storefront and buy some Gypsy robes and earrings! Call yourself Madame Olga.

"What do poets really want?" I was asked that once by a clever professor of philosophy. It was late at night and we were drinking a lot of wine, so I just said the first thing that came into my mind: "They want to know about things that cannot be put into words."

An object is an encyclopedia of archetypes. I've learned that writing "The Broom."

Ambiguity is the world's condition. Poetry flirts with ambiguity. As a "picture of reality" it is truer than any other. Ambiguity is. This doesn't mean you're supposed to write poems no one understands.

Metaphor offers the opportunity for my inwardness to connect itself with the world out there. All things are related, and that knowledge resides in my unconscious.

The poets and writers I admire stood alone. Philosophy, too, is always alone. Poetry and philosophy make slow solitary readers.

God died and we were left with Emerson. Some are still milking Emerson's cow, but there are problems with that milk.

A recent critic has enumerated what he calls "the lexicon" of recent poetry. The words mentioned as occurring repeatedly are: wings, stones, silence, breath, snow, blood, water, light, bones, roots, jewels, glass, absence, sleep, darkness. The accusation is that the words are used as mere ornaments. It doesn't occur to the critic that these words could have an intense life for a mind with an imaginative and even a philosophical bent.

The worst offense one can commit in a poem is humor. Irony and wit are acceptable, but laughter in a lyric poem is a serious transgression. Great art, or so people think, is serious business. The more solemn the tone, the worthier of respect it is. Plato censored poetry that provokes "frivolous laughter," and so do my students reading Frank O'Hara.

Imagism is realism minus the moral. If Imagist poems were didactic, people would find them more acceptable.

Here's the moralist definition of "the beautiful": Not life as it is, but life as it ought to be.

What John Gardner in his *Moral Fiction* doesn't get is that the history of Western literature is really a long quarrel between the poet and the priest, the poet and the schoolteacher.

How to communicate consciousness . . . the present moment lived intensely that language locked in the temporal order of the sentence cannot reproduce?

Time is the lapse between perception and recognition (consciousness of that perception).

The last hundred years of literary history have proved that there are a number of contradictory and yet, nevertheless, successful ways of writing a poem. What do Whitman, Dickinson, Baudelaire, Rimbaud, Yeats, Williams, and Stevens have in common? Plenty, and nothing at all.

Poem: A theater in which one is the auditorium, the stage, the sets, the actors, the author, the public, the critic. All at once!

Myth: Finding a hidden plot in a metaphor. There's a story and a cosmology in every great metaphor.

I love the saying "No two eggs are alike."

There are critics unable to experience the figurative, the way some people are color-blind and tone-deaf, or lack a sense of humor. They can tell it's a metaphor, but it doesn't do anything for them. If it cannot be paraphrased, this then becomes a further proof that it's completely worthless.

Metaphor proves the existence of Heaven and Hell.

Ideological criticism is always stationary. It has its "true position," from which it doesn't budge. It's like insisting that all paintings should be viewed from a distance of ten feet and only ten feet. Many paintings do not fully exist at that distance, of course. Besides, one is never at a single vantage point except intellectually. In life and in art one is simultaneously in several places at once.

It is the object I'm watching, the fork, for example, which sets up the rules of its visibility.

The modern poem implies a modern aesthetics and philosophy. Poetry written in that mode cannot be understood without an understanding of modern intellectual history. This seems pretty obvious, but not to everyone. Many of our leading literary critics have not read as widely as our poets. The poets' readings are much more adventurous. And then, of course, there's painting and cinema, which the critics customarily forget.

It goes without saying that a Chinese has a greater appreciation of Chinese poetry than a Westerner. But poetry is not only what stays in the cultural context, but what transcends it.

The theory of archetypes: Inside is where we meet everyone else; it's on the outside that we are truly alone.

Two ways of creating: To uncover what is already there or to make something entirely new. My problem is that I believe in both.

"Momentary deities" is, I believe, how the Greeks thought of words.

Consciousness: Separating "I" from "it." The "I" can be spoken but not the "it."

"He has great images," we used to say, and we meant that the poet kept surprising us by his wild associations. Total freedom of the imagination was our ideal then. That's all we loved and demanded from the poetry we were going to write.

Beautiful, mysterious images are static. Too many such images clog the poem. A mysterious image is a holy, wonder-working icon. How many of those can you have in a single poem?

The inventor of the modern metaphor, Arthur Rimbaud, regarded himself as a seer. He saw that the secret ambition of a radical metaphor is metaphysical. It could open new worlds. It could touch the absolute. He gave up poetry when he began to doubt that truth.

Most poets do not understand their own metaphors.

I proclaim the hermeneutics of the perfectly clear. Its ambition is to find hidden opacities in the brightest sunlight.

Nietzsche: "A small overstrained animal whose days are numbered" proposes the "object of its love." That's what my poems are about.

Contemporary poets have for the most part forgotten about symbolism, especially its one great insight that Being cannot be stated but only hinted at.

It's curious that there are still critics who equate imagination and fantasy.

Certain philosophers have understood the poetic image better than literary critics. Bachelard, Heidegger, and Ricoeur come to mind. They grasped its epistemological and metaphysical ambition. The critics too often see the image solely in literary terms.

What a mess! I believe in images as vehicles of transcendence, but I don't believe in God!

Heisenberg's "uncertainty principle" has comic potential, besides being the best formulation of the comic spirit.

"We understand others as a result of the speed with which we pass over words," says Valéry. This describes for me what happens in a free verse poem. One speeds up, or one slows down the flow of words. One pauses . . . One says nothing . . . Then, one resumes one's pace.

The common object is the sphinx, whose riddle the contemplative poet must solve.

J. Riddel: "What is it the poet reaches? Not mere knowledge. He obtains entrance into the relationship of word and thing."

Beware of synchronicity—"the meaningful coincidence of an external event with an inner motive." That way madness lies.

The provincialism of our criticism: One reads B and Y, but not Z, D, or N. One has an extremely narrow knowledge of the field, yet nevertheless likes to generalize about American poetry.

"The Triumph of Pere Ubu," an essay on History and Stupidity. That would be something!

"Truth eludes the methodical man," says Gadamer. Thank God! That's why poets have a chance.

Poe: "The word 'infinity,' like the words 'God' and 'spirit,' is by no means the expression of an idea, but an effort at one."

What to call "It?" You need a word. You need several words for the ineffable.

Here's what I understand to be the spirit of Dada: Gentle, kind, most indulgent and benevolent reader, friend of friends, brother and sister of my soul, kiss my ass!

Form is "timing"—the exact amount of silence necessary between words and images to make them meaningful. The stand-up comedians know all about that.

Poe in *Eureka*: "Space and duration are one." Space is the image of Time in the moment of consciousness.

The fate of the poet is the fate of the soul in every man and woman.

I always had the clearest sense that a lot of people out there would have killed me if given an opportunity. It's a long list. Stalin, Hitler, Mao are on it, of course. And that's only our century! The Catholic Church, the Puritans, the Moslems, etc., etc. I represent what has always been joyfully exterminated.

Note to future historians: Don't read old issues of *The New York Times*. Read the poets.

Time is the subjective *par excellence*. Objectively, time doesn't exist, despite the appearances. This is Gurdjieff's idea, which fascinated my father.

Imagism is about the passion for accuracy. To get it right, etc. But, it's not easy to get "it" right! A philosophical problem. Imagism is the epistemology of modern poetry.

A metaphysics without a self and without a God! Is that what you want, Simic?

"The iron hand of necessity shaking the dicebox of chance." I believe that's Nietzsche's phrase. I've been worrying about it for years.

The most profound thing that Emerson said about the poet is that he knows the Secret of the World: that Being passes into Appearance, and Unity into Variety.

I have an idea for a new game of chess in which the value of each figure would change from move to move. Pawns could become knights, the king could turn into a queen, and so on. The choice would be the player's. His opponent would have to anticipate all the additional options. A game of infinite and dizzying complexity.

A poem is a place where affinities are discovered. Poetry is a way of thinking through affinities.

The cookie-cutter poets. The cookie-cutters are made of gold and sit under glass in their grandparents' parlors.

I like the folksy vulgarity of Chaucer, Rabelais, and Cervantes.

There are poets who treat you like an imbecile, and there are poets who treat you like a poet.

"The greatest danger to the poem is the poetic." I don't remember who said that.

What the political right and left have in common is their hatred of modern art and literature. Come to think of it, all the churches hate it, too, which doesn't leave us many supporters. On the one hand we have the dopey rich who collect Andy Warhol's soup cans, and on the other hand some poor kid in love with the poems of Russell Edson and Sylvia Plath. Oh boy!

Everything was right with the world until that yokel Rimbaud opened his mouth.

To the narrative poets: What do you think Pound meant when he said, "Do not retell in mediocre verse what has already been done in good prose"?

Everybody wants to be able to paraphrase the content of the poem, except the poet.

The encounter between philosophy and poetry, my little lambs, is not a tragedy but a sublime comedy.

IV

The poet is like a compulsive talker at a funeral. People nudge him and tell him to be quiet and he apologizes, agrees that this is not the place, and so on and so forth as he goes on blabbering.

Cioran writes, "God is afraid of man. . . . Man is a monster, and history has proved it."

My ideal is Robert Burton's *The Anatomy of Melancholy*, a catalog of many varieties of mopiness human beings are subject to, everything from the gloom caused by the evils of the world to the kind caused by lovers' squabbles. Burton, who is one of the great stylists in the language, wrote the book to relieve his own low spirits. The result is the most cheerful book on general unhappiness we have.

"A book suitable for reading in an abandoned house among weeds on a still night and a full stomach," writes Felisberto Hernandez, who once described a young woman about to recite one of her poems as assuming an attitude that made one think of something between infinity and a sneeze.

In no other century, in no other literature of the past has the image been this important. In the age of ideology and advertisement, the poet, too, trusts the eyes more than the ear.

No preconceived aesthetic sense can guide the poet and the artist in American cities, where chance rules.

In poetry, to quote a bluesman who calls himself Satan, one must "learn to do wrong with respect."

The soul squawking to the body about its days being numbered. That's what most blues songs and lyric poems are about.

Collage is a mystic's medium.

I'm a jailbird from every Garden of Eden, every Utopia that has ever been imagined.

"The future will be post-individualist," the critic Frederic Jameson tells us. Whether it'll be Stalin's, Hitler's, or Mao's model, he doesn't say.

Things, do you know suffering? The mystery of the object is the mystery of a closed door. The object is the place where the real and the imaginary collide.

Ars poetica: I ate the white chickens and left the red wheelbarrow out in the rain.

As a poet, the Lord of the Universe is hopelessly obscure.

Intense experience eludes language. Language is the Fall from the awe and consciousness of being.

To be a poet is to feel something like a unicyclist in a desert, a pornographic magician performing in the corner of the church during Mass, a drag queen attending night classes and blowing kisses at the teacher.

The prose poem is a fabulous beast like the sphinx. A monster made up of prose and poetry.

A horror movie for vegetarians: Greasy sausages kept falling from the sky into people's bean soup.

"They are bad for you," my friends tell me. As if all that stands between me and immortality are a couple of Italian sausages.

She is a passionate multiculturalist except when it comes to ethnic food. This is where she draws the line. If these minorities could learn to forgo deep-fried foods, she could open her heart to them even more.

In the school of virtue, I'm still five years old. I want to sit in some woman's lap and suck her breast, but they won't let me. Give me my thumb to chew at least, I protest! But they sprinkle hot chili sauce on all my fingers and order me to stand in the corner.

American unhappiness has no history because history has to do with real events and not with a Dream.

How is it that certain expressions of our own subjectivity in poetry strike the reader as merely self-indulgent or sentimental, while others, equally personal, have a universal resonance? The answer may be that there are two kinds of poets: Those who ask the reader to wallow in self-pity with them and those who simply remind them of their common human predicament.

To rescue the banal is every lyric poet's ambition.

All lives are strange, but the lives of immigrants and exiles are even more so. My parents died a long way from where they were born. It's not how they imagined their lives were going to be. Even at the age of eighty-eight in a nursing home in Dover, New Hampshire, my mother was puzzled. What does it all mean, she wanted to know? What terrified her was the likelihood that it meant nothing.

Our conservatives and liberals both dream of censorship. Their ideal, without them realizing it, is Mao's China. Only a few books in bookstores and libraries, and every one of them carrying a wholesome message.

American academics suffer from cultural insecurity. They really don't know who they are, but our writers do, and that's the problem.

"She faked orgasm each time she masturbated," writes an unknown wit in a tabloid.

My father's comment on an old waiter in our favorite Greek restaurant: "His grandpa ran the shadow projector in Plato's Cave."

"I would have given my pants for . . . ," he kept shouting all his life.

Some readers find my poems obscure because, well, I don't sum it up for them. That is to say, I have too much respect for them to play the preacher, but that's what they want from their poets.

My student Jeff McRae says, "Life at its best is a beautiful sadness."

To me the test of a literary theory is what it has to say about the lyric poem. If it avoids the lyric or stumbles over it, I say forget it. It's a fraud.

Here's the first rule of insomnia: Don't talk to the heroes and villains on the screen.

Memory: Not my own. Whose then? At 4 a.m., when the heart skips a beat or two, I saw myself with arms spread on the gallows about to address a huge crowd and found no words in my mouth.

Years later, when some of my high school teachers in Yugoslavia were told that I had graduated from the university, they just laughed and refused to believe any of it.
    "That lazy bum? Never in a thousand years."
    My mother took an equally dim view. "He'll end up in prison," she told everybody.
    I don't think she ever truly believed I was actually a professor at a university. He's lying to me, she thought, or he has them all hoodwinked in some way, but is bound to be found out sooner or later.

In the beginning there were Whitman and Dickinson and Poe. Whitman was our Homer and Dickinson our Sappho, but who the hell was Poe?

The aim of ideologies of ethnicity, nationality, religion, and gender is to remove the sense of one's own individual limitations and failure as a human being and to replace the "I" by a "we."

The best recommendation for wine, tobacco, sex and loose talk is that every so-called moral majority is against them.

The often-heard assertion that there's no truth outside of language is just jive.

Our rich are torn between self-pity (they're paying too much in taxes) and self-adulation. To live without excuses is now a profoundly un-American attitude.

He kissed ass so much his brain had turdified.

Even birds detest poetry, it seems. The beauty of the sunset over the quiet lake made them holler. Even the leaves, shushing each other into sleep, grew agitated. The grandeur of the sky lasted just as long as it took them to make their complaints, and then they were done.

The identification of what remains untouched by change has been the philosopher's task. Art and literature, on the contrary, have been delighted with the ephemeral— the smell of bread, for instance.

Centuries ago, when the king's advisers and seers gave wrong predictions as to the outcome of military campaigns, they were tortured and publicly executed. In our days, they continue being called "experts" and appear on TV.

Deterrence by example. Let's bomb X so that Y and Z will realize we mean business and behave. By that logic, why not hang a few crooked politicians and bankers so that others may be warned?

Always the foreigner, the stranger, someone a bit fishy. Even the smiling dummies in store windows eyed me with suspicion today.

Rubbing against so many strangers in so many places and aping their ways to pass for a native has made you incomprehensible even to yourself.

"We lost everything," my mother used to say. She was right. Everything we ever had in terms of possessions and identities was no more. One day we were folks next door and the next we were riffraff without a country.

Nietzsche: "That the lie is permitted as means to pious ends is a part of the theory of every priesthood."

American writers have been lucky that the rich and powerful have had no interest in making them their concubines. Our so-called intellectuals have not been so fortunate.

The unbelievers say with the scientists that the morning light has no consciousness; the believers know it does.

Orphan factories and scapegoat farms are the Balkans' chief economy.

Wary of every enthusiasm, ready to run away at the first opportunity. Only on the subject of the absolute scumminess of politicians do I feel completely confident.

At night frequently I have the same dream: A border guard steps with his boot on my passport.

63

How to kill a lot of people and sleep like a baby continues to be the statesman's ideal. That's why he needs intellectuals to divide murderers into good and bad, to explain that we are doing evil to these people for their own good. Brutality and violence always require a new, superior morality.

Nationalism is the love of the smell of our collective shit.

Any ideology or belief that doesn't have hatred as spice has no chance of becoming popular. To be a true believer you have to be a champion hater.

Here's my contribution to the politics of nostalgia: The servants of the rich (our politicians and journalists) should wear doorman's uniforms. Let flunkies be instantly recognized from the distance, as in the old days.

The silent laughing chorus behind all ideas of progress.

Every poetic image asks why is there something rather than nothing, as it renews our astonishment that things exist.

There's a tradition of wonderful misfits in literature, unclassifiable writers and poets, like Michaux and Edson, suspicious of literature, who are at the same time its biggest addicts. Only a style that is a carnival of styles seems to please them. A poetry, in short, that has the feel of the circus, a sideshow, vaudeville, facts stranger than fiction, fake miracles and superstitions, dream books sold at supermarket counters, etc.

I never "write." I just tinker.

The prose poem is like a dog that talks.

It is possible to make astonishingly tasty dishes from the simplest ingredients. That's my aesthetics. I'm the poet of the frying pan and my love's little toes.

To preserve the standpoint of the individual is the continuous struggle. The tribe is always trying to reform you, teach you some manners and a new vocabulary.

For any conspiracy theory history is a sham. Every public event is a guise behind which true events take place. Conspiracy, in that sense, is a theory of representation. What you see is really not what is truly there.

Free will is an illusion. In conspiracy theory, the law of gravity is absolute. Planes cannot fly.

The world is always old. There are no new events because conspiracy is eternal.

Conspiracy is the only true theology. All other theologies are part of the great conspiracy.

You think all this is funny? Your laughter, Simic, is a sign of foolishness. You're a dupe, a gullible hayseed when it comes to the dark forces of conspiracy playing all around you.

Wittgenstein Bubble Gum: Trying to say that which cannot be said. Endeavoring, exerting myself daily—and how!—to woo, to throw a net over, to grapple and scuffle with that which cannot be voiced, intoned, ventriloquized as to its content, even in a ghastly stammer, and is, perhaps, given only in small hints by a hand gesture, a shrugged shoulder, a long sigh. Humdinger! Language is a monkey wrench.

American identify is really about having many identities simultaneously. We came to America to escape our old identities, which the multiculturalists now wish to restore to us.

The muses are cooks. Poetry is a kind of cookery. I divide my poems between appetizers, stews, and desserts.

On the invisible line between sayable and the unsay-able—the lyric poem.

If music is about the use of time and painting about the use of space, in lyric poems they're brought together. Image brings space into language (time), which the language then fragments into space.

Poetry like the movies worries about sequence, framing, montage, and cutting.

Not all innocent victims qualify as innocents, I've concluded, reading the daily papers for the last forty years. The ethnic group has first to become fashionable as an object of pity before their innocence as victims is accepted. Otherwise, forget it.

Stupidity is having a national revival. All you need to do is turn on the TV to see its big, friendly smile.

A fierce competition is in progress as to who is the biggest victim among us. Right now, the children of privilege are winning and the poor and the unlettered are losing. Money buys even victimhood.

A poem like a holy icon, painted in secret hope that some day a god may come to inhabit it miraculously.

Didn't Joyce call poetry "soul butter" somewhere?

I miss phrenology. It would be nice to have someone feel the bumps on the heads of our presidential candidates while they address the nation.

Ambrose Bierce: "That immortal ass, the average man."

It's getting dark and I'm showing my teeth to the hell-hound running behind me on the road to nowhere.

Soon we'll all be returning to Emily Dickinson's dark closet. Funambulist of the invisible, make it quick, start your walk.

The ideal place to teach creative writing is a used bookstore, says my friend Vava Hristic.

I'm writing for a school of philosophers who will feast, who will be remembered for asking for a third and fourth helping of the same dish while discussing metaphysics. Philosophers who seek those moments in which the senses, the mind, and the emotions are experienced together.

My hunch that language is inadequate when speaking about experience is really a religious idea, what they call negative theology.

The ambition of much of today's literary theory seems to be to find ways to read literature without imagination.

What all reformers and builders of utopias share is the fear of the comic. They are right. Laughter undermines discipline and leads to anarchy. Humor is anti-utopian. There was more truth in jokes Soviets told than in all the books written on the USSR.

My old poems on Geometry ("The Point," "Triangle," "Euclid Avenue," "The Ballad of the Wheel") are my attempt to read between Euclid's lines.

New York City is much too complex a place for just one god and one devil.

The most original achievement of American literature is the absence of an official literary language.

Where time and eternity intersect my consciousness is the traffic cop holding up a STOP sign.

Ethics of reading. Does the critic have any moral responsibility toward the author's intentions? Of course not, say all the hip critics. What about the translator? Isn't the critic, too, a translator? Would we accept a translation of Dante's *Divine Comedy* which would disregard the poet's intentions?

Gombrowicz, too, used to wonder, how is it that good students understand novels and poems, while literary critics mostly talk nonsense.

The ambition of literary realism is to plagiarize God's creation.

Seeing is determined not by the eye but by the clarity of my consciousness. Most of the time the eyes see nothing.

In their effort to divorce language and experience, deconstructionist critics remind me of middle-class parents who do not allow their children to play in the street.

Lately in the United States we have been caught between critics who do not believe in literature and writers who believe only in naïve realism. Imagination continues to be what everybody pretends does not exist.

Many of our critics read literature like totalitarian cops on the lookout for subversive material—for instance, the claim that there is a world outside language.

Poetry tries to bridge the abyss lying between the name and the thing. That language is a problem is no news to poets.

Poets worth reading usually believe things the age they live in no longer does. Poets are always anachronistic, obsolete, unfashionable, and permanently contemporary.

Can a timeless moment of consciousness ever be adequately conveyed in a medium that depends on time, i.e., language? This is the mystic's and the lyric poet's problem.

A good-tasting homemade stew of angel and beast.

One point of agreement between Eastern and Western philosophy: men live like fools.

Wisdom as measure, as a sense of proportion, as middle ground. If it's defined that way, one sees why there are only a few examples of wisdom in the entire history of the world.

If Derrida is right, all that the poets have ever done is whistle in the dark.

Like many others, I grew up in an age that preached liberty and built slave camps. Consequently, reformers of all varieties terrify me. I only need to be told that I'm being served a new, improved, low-fat baked ham, and I gag.

It's the desire for irreverence as much as anything else that brought me first to poetry. The need to make fun of authority, break taboos, celebrate the body and its functions, claim that one has seen angels in the same breath as one says that there is no god. Just thinking about the possibility of saying shit to everything made me roll on the floor with happiness.

Here's Octavio Paz at his best: "The poem will continue to be one of the few resources by which man can go beyond himself to find out what he is profoundly and originally."

The sense of myself existing comes first. Then come images and then language.

Being is not an idea in philosophy, but a wordless experience we have from time to time.

Suppose you don't believe in either Hobbes's notion that man is evil and society is good, or Rousseau's that man is good and society evil. Suppose you believe in the hopeless and messy mixture of everything.

I know a fellow who reads modern poetry only in the john.

Here's a quick recipe on how to make a modern poem out of an old one. Just take out the beginning and the end; the invocation to the Muses and the nicely wrapped up final message.

I still think Camus was right. Heroic lucidity in the face of the absurd is about all we really have.

Fourier, who planned a model of perfect human society, was known never to laugh. There you have it! Collective happiness under the steely gaze of a murderer.

A true confession: I believe in a soluble fish.

A school where the best students are always kicked out, there you have the history of the academy's relationship to contemporary art and literature. (I think Valéry said something like that.)

The prose poem is the result of two contradictory

impulses, prose and poetry, and therefore cannot exist, but it does. This is the sole instance we have of squaring the circle.

First you simplify whatever is complex, you reduce reality to a single concept, and then you start a church of some kind. What surprises me endlessly is how every new absolutism, every one-sided worldview is instantly attractive to so many seemingly intelligent people.

My soul is constituted of thousands of images I cannot erase. Everything I remember vividly, from a fly on the wall in Belgrade to some street in San Francisco early one morning. I'm a grainy old, often silent, often flickering film.

Only poetry can measure the distance between ourselves and the Other.

Form in a poem is like the order of performing acts in a circus.

One writes because one has been touched by the yearning for and the despair of ever touching the Other.

We call "street wise" someone who knows how to look, listen, and interpret the teeming life around him. To walk down a busy city block is a critical act. Literature, aesthetics, and psychology all come into play.

Nationalists and religious fundamentalists all hate the modern city because of its variety and spontaneity. Stupidity and ill will easily rule in a small community, but in a city one has many ways of eluding their grasp.

Hopscotch. Pierre leapt from Stalin to Mao to Pol Pot to Saddam. I hope after the experience of this century that no one in the future will still believe in the myth of the critical independence of the intellectuals.

The lyric poem is often a scandalous assertion that the private is public, that the local is universal, that the ephemeral is eternal. And it happens! The poets turn out to be right. This is what the philosophers cannot forgive the poets.

How many literary theorists and teachers of literature truly understand that poems are not written merely for the sake of oneself, or for the sake of some idea, or for the sake of the reader, but out of a deep reverence for the old and noble art of poetry.

We speak of rhyme as a memory aid, but not of striking images and unusual similitudes that have a way of making themselves impossible to forget.

I love Mina Loy's "No man whose sex life was satisfactory ever became a moral censor."

Since democracy does not believe in the exclusive possession of truth by one party, it is incompatible with nationalism and religion, I tell my Yugoslav friends.

My aspiration is to create a kind of nongenre made up of fiction, autobiography, the essay, poetry, and of course, the joke!

A theory of the universe: the whole is mute; the part screams with pain or guffaws.

I would like to write a book that would be a meditation on all kinds of windows. Store windows, monastic windows, windows struck by sunlight on a street of dark windows, windows in which clouds are reflected, imaginary windows, hotel windows, prison windows . . . windows one peeks out of or peeks in. Windows that have the quality of religious art, etc.

Rushdie's case proves that literature is the dangerous activity, not literary criticism and its currently fashionable notion that literature is merely the propaganda of the ruling ideology.

Here's the totalitarian theory of literature from Plato to the Inquisition to Stalin and all their followers:

1. Separation of content and form, ideas from experience. Literature is primarily its content.
2. The content needs to be unmasked, revealed for what it truly is. The cop slapping the young poet and demanding to know who ordered him to write like that is the secret ideal.
3. Literature is clever propaganda for a particular cause.
4. Literature on its own terms is socially dangerous. Pure art is a blasphemy against authority.
5. The poet and the writer are never to be trusted. Trust the critic and the censor for their constant vigilance.

What is the difference between a reader and a critic? The reader identifies with the work of literature, the critic keeps a distance in order to see the shape it makes. The

74

reader is after pleasure, the critic wants to understand how it works. The erotic and the hermeneutic are often at odds and yet they should be companions.

A New Hampshire high school student reading an ancient Chinese poem and being moved—a theory of literature that cannot account for that commonplace miracle is worthless.

Another large group of cultural illiterates we are stuck with: college professors who do not read contemporary literature or know modern art, modern music, theater, cinema, jazz, etc.

Eternity is the insomnia of Time. Did somebody say that, or is it my idea?

If poems were the expression of one's ethnicity they could remain local, but they are written by individuals in all cultures, which makes them universal.

Both imagination and the experience of consciousness affirm that each is all and all is each. Metaphors (seeing resemblance everywhere) are internationalist in spirit. If I were a nationalist, I'd prohibit the use of a metaphor.

For Emily Dickinson every philosophical idea was a potential lover. Metaphysics is the realm of eternal seduction of the spirit by ideas.

The individual is the measurer, the world is what is measured, and the language of poetry is the measure. There! Now you can hang me by my tongue!

How do we know the Other? By being madly in love.

Comes a time when the living moment expands. The instant becomes roomy. It opens up. Suddenly everything inside and outside of ourselves is utterly different. I know what I am, and I know what I am not. It's just me and It.

Is the clarity of consciousness the negation of imagination? One can imagine plenty in a state of semi-consciousness.

The highest levels of consciousness are wordless and its lowest gabby.

The tribe always wants you to write about "great and noble subjects."

When I was little, bad boys in my neighborhood advised me to grab my balls every time I saw a priest. It's the first lesson in the arts I was given.

Seeing the familiar with new eyes, that quintessential idea of modern art and literature, the exile and the immigrant experience daily.

Here's Konstantin Nojka's observation, with which I agree completely: "Thought precedes the word—as in the example of a little kid who calls a strange man 'dad.' The adults correct him and say it's not daddy, but what the kid means is that he's like dad—has the same height, glasses, etc."

The academics always believe that they have read more than the poets, but this has rarely been my experience. Poets of my generation and the preceding generation are far better read than their academic contemporaries, with exceptions, of course, on both sides.

Christ, like Sappho, challenges the tribe. Their message is, you have no tribal obligations, only love for the Father in the first case and love of your own solitude in the second.

Consciousness: this dying match that sees and knows the name of what it throws its brief light upon.

Imagination equals Eros. I want to experience what it's like to be inside someone else in the moment when that someone is being touched by me.

I'm in the business of translating what cannot be translated: being and its silence.

Ars Poetica: trying to make your jailers laugh.

Two young birch trees wrestling in the wind. The crow in the snow refereeing.

Here where they make piggy banks with the face of Jesus.

Strafford, New Hampshire, Orpheus assuaging the fierceness of wild beasts with his new kazoo.

The day I went to make funeral arrangements for my

father-in-law, I caught a glimpse of the mortician's wife nursing the mortician's new daughter. Her breasts were swollen huge with milk.

A sequel to Dante's *Divine Comedy:* The modern hero retraces his steps from heaven to hell.

I have a House of Horrors the size of my head, or the size of the known universe. It doesn't matter which.

Like everybody else, I'm betting everything on the remote possibility that one of many lies will come true. I say to myself in moments of tenderness, perhaps you're more of a philosopher than you know.

As for the ALWAYS OPEN, always brightly lit House of Horrors, it's just a windowless room, empty except for some trash on the floor.

The Gestapo and the KGB were also convinced that the personal is political. Virtue by decree was their other belief.

The closeness of two people listening together to music they both love. There's no more perfect union. I remember a summer evening, a good bottle of white wine, and Helen and I listening to Prez play "Blue Lester." We were so attentive, as only those who have heard a piece a hundred times can be, so this time it seemed the piece lasted forever.

The lost thread of a dream. What a pretty phrase!

Cioran is right when he says that "we are all religious spirits without a religion."

Eurocentrism is the dumbest idea ever proposed by academics. The notion that all European history—all its philosophy, literature, art, cuisine, martyrdom, oppression—is the expression of a single ideology belongs in *The National Enquirer* on the same page with "I Was Bigfoot's Loveslave."

Even as I concentrate all my attention on the fly on the table, I glance fleetingly at myself.

America is the only country in the world where a rich woman with servants can speak of being a woman oppressed and not be laughed at.

What the lyric poets want is to convert their fragment of time into eternity. It's like going to the bank and expecting to get a million dollars for your nickel.

I agree with Isaiah Berlin when he says in an interview, "I do not find all-embracing systems congenial." I have a horror of minds who see all events as instances of universal rules and principles. I believe in the deep-set messiness of everything. I associate tidiness with dictatorship.

How to kill the innate poetry of children—the secret agenda of a conference on primary school education. I met teachers who fear poetry the way vampires fear the cross.

For a man like Teller, science meant new and much-improved ways of killing people, and he was enthusiastically received in high places.

It is in the works of art and literature that one has the richest experience of the Other. When the experience is truly powerful, we can be anybody, a nineteenth-century Russian prince, a fifteenth-century Italian harlot.

Most of our political writers on the left and the right are interchangeable. That's why it was child's play for so many liberals to become neoconservatives. What serenity the day one realizes that!

Here's one firm law of history: Truth is known at precisely that point in time when nobody gives a shit.

A poem is an invitation to a voyage. As in life, we travel to see fresh sights.

To be an exception to the rule is my sole ambition.

Twenty years ago the poem for me was still mostly an inspired and unpremeditated utterance. My friend Vasko Popa on the other hand, was all calculation. A poem was an act of supreme critical intelligence for him. He had already thought out everything he was going to write for the rest of his life. Once late at night, after much wine, he described to me in detail his future poems. He wasn't putting me on. In later years I'd see these poems come into print one by one, and they were just as he described them that night.

Popa's metaphysics was Symbolist, and yet it's not so much that he used symbols in his poetry, and he did. What he really wanted to understand is the secret of how symbols are made. Poetry is sacred action, it's been said. Popa's poems demonstrate how the laws of the imagination work.

"The salad bird" writes Lucian, "is an enormous bird covered all over with salad greens instead of feathers; its wings look exactly like lettuce leaves." For Popa, language was not an abstract system but a living idiom, an idiom already full of poetic invention. In that respect, his imagination and his poetry are wholly determined by the language in which he wrote. In his poems the reader enters the Serbian language and meets the gods and demons hiding there.

Little said, much meant, is what poetry is all about. An idiom is the lair of the tribal beast. It carries its familiar smell. We are here in the realm of the submerged and elusive meanings that do not correspond to any actual word on the page. Lyricism, in its truest sense, is the awe before the untranslatable. Like childhood, it is a language that cannot be replaced by any other language. A great lyric poem must approach untranslatability.

Translation is an actor's medium. If I cannot make myself believe that I'm writing the poem I'm translating, no degree of aesthetic admiration for the work can help me. The philosophical clear-sightedness of a man who is taking a long siesta on a day when many important matters should be attended to. As somebody said, cats know laziness is divine.

Blues musicians do not doubt that music touches the soul.

My poem "Midpoint" is a reduction, the cutting down to

a kind of algebraic equation of a ten-page poem on cities where I have lived. The paring down occurred when I realized that all my future cities are the ghost images of the city where I was born. In my imagination I'm always at midpoint.

To be bilingual is to realize that the name and the thing are not bound intrinsically. It is possible to find oneself in a dark hole between languages. I experience this now when I speak Serbian, which I no longer speak fluently. I go expecting to find a word, knowing that there was a word there once, and find instead a hole and a silence.

I grew up among some very witty people, I now realize. They knew how to tell stories and how to laugh and that has made all the difference.

The restaurant is Greek. The waiter's name is Socrates, so Plato must be in the kitchen, and Aristotle is the fellow studying a racing form at the cash register.

Today's special: Grilled calamari with fresh parsley, garlic, and olive oil.

When I started writing poetry in 1955 all the girls I wanted to show my poems to were American. I was stuck. It was never possible for me to write in my native language.

I prefer Aristophanes to Sophocles, Rabelais to Dante. There's as much truth in laughter as there is in tragedy, a view not shared by many people. They still think of comedy as nose-thumbing at the serious things in life.

My second-grade teacher in Belgrade told me more than forty-five years ago that I was a "champion liar." I still remember being mortally offended and kind of flattered.

Only through poetry can human solitude be heard in the history of humanity. In that respect, all the poets who ever wrote are contemporaries.

A scene from French movies of the fifties that I still love: A fly gets shut in a room with three armed thugs and a woman, gagged and bound, who watches them with eyes popping. In front of each man on the table there is a sugar cube and a pile of large bills. No one stirs. A naked bulb hangs from the ceiling by a long wire so they can see the fly count its legs. It counts them on the table, tantalizingly close to a sugar cube, and then it counts them at the end of someone's nose.

I have no idea if this is the way it really was in the movie. I've worked on the scene over the years, making little adjustments in it as one does with a poem.

My life is at the mercy of my poetry.

I thought "nosology" had to do with noses. Something like a science of noses. Many noses coming to be examined. The perfect nose in the lobby of a grand hotel lighting a gold-tipped cigarette behind a potted palm. The pretty nosologist examining my nose and almost touching it with her own.

Nosology, unfortunately, has nothing to do with noses.

O beau pays! The monkey at the typewriter.

In a neighborhood frequented by muggers and rapists after dark, I bring out my soapbox and shout: "Everything I have ever said has been completely misunderstood!"

In a room with a noisy window-fan I'm reading Meister Eckhart's sermon, the one in which he says: "The moment in which God made the first man and the moment in which the last man will disappear, and the moment in which I'm speaking are all one and the same moment."
    Little ideas and big ideas are buzzing in my head when I look up from the book and see my grim face looking back at me from the mirror across the room.

Thoreau loved ants. He'd meet one in the morning and spend the whole day talking to him. Poe often dreamed he was a black pullet pecking in the graveyard on moonlit nights. Hawthorne kept a rusty nail in his shoe as a pet. Melville nursed his melancholy by eating fresh strawberries in cream on summer mornings. Come evening, Emily Dickinson could see the shadow her brain cast on the bedroom wall. Whitman's beard once caught fire. The firemen came from as far as Louisiana to put it out. Emerson said, "The world is an immense picture book." "Everybody's using its pages to wipe his ass," wrote in response an unknown American genius in the margin of my library book.

The air is full of flying cinders this morning. Whole neighborhoods could be going up in flames while the children chase each other in the playground, while they kick the one fallen against the high, peeling wall of the school they go to and scream in mock terror, fleeing the girl with crossed eyes. All that, mind you, behind a rusty fence firmly secured with a chain and a heavy padlock.

The windows of Hotel du Nord have a view of the snows of Labrador that are famous for their yellow sunflowers. The white paint in our room is peeling; the old beds and chairs have gone to China to be missionaries; the desk clerk is as deaf as a shoe brush. When somebody knocked, we ran to open. There was never anyone there. The quiet that reigns in the hotel is like that of an Egyptian pyramid in a hundred-year-old postcard with an address in Oklahoma on the other side.

The sky is blue and so is the ceiling. Glued to the wall, there's a cutout of a blonde child pointing to a picture of a camel that could have come out of a long-discontinued breakfast cereal. Over him, hung from a silver rod by a metal hook, there's a postage stamp with a picture of another smaller child dressed in a Renaissance costume. This one appears to be saying his bedtime prayer. Their father, the prince, has gone off to stand on the parapet with his beard and hair dripping red paint.

If the night ever falls, we will light matches and invite the children to be our guests at a meal of watch wheels and watch faces.

The kid torturing the cat next door has a great future in store for him. His mama loves him, his daddy does too. They live in a pretty white house, with two columns. Their trimmed hedges and trees keep their sober dignity even when I yell for him to stop.

He sits on his back steps lonely, sweet-looking

and idle. The cat is nowhere to be seen. The weather is beautiful.

Angelic birdseed on the tip of Martha's pink tongue while she speaks of her faith in God's benevolence.

It was the first day of spring. Birds were singing. Romeo loved the smell of his shit, but when he smelled Juliet's rose-scented farts, he ran out on the balcony screaming, "Give me air!"

Old man eating soup with his hat on, slurping and wiping his mouth with a sleeve while pointing with the spoon at the crows sitting on the top of a white church. "Like the devil himself," he says, "Yes, sir, like the devil himself."

In a zoo I noticed many animals who had a fleeting resemblance to me.

"Dear Comrade Stalin," he wrote, "my dream is to see the whole world become a collective poultry farm."

At Nick's, today's special was bean soup with sausage. You could hear everybody ordering it, even the bag lady we often saw sleeping in doorways.
"I used to read palms for a living," she told me with her mouth full. And then, taking a swig from a brown paper bag from under the table, "Lift your hand, everybody, so that I may read your future."

The evening is coming. Someone milks a black cow. Someone reloads a different gun at the fair and fires.

"*Return of the Invisible Man* is on the late show," someone says as he bends down to pick a wild poppy in the darkening meadow.

As the curtain goes up, there's a gasp of surprise and terror from the audience. The lovers on the stage have two heads on the same shoulder. They're sitting in the same chair at the same round table, gazing at each other lovingly.

People rarely doubt what they see, more often they doubt what they think, says one head to the other. We in the audience are too busy counting the lovers' eyes and noses to listen to their words.

The twelve girls in the gospel chorus sang as if dogs were biting their asses.

A dream: In a burning house I'm reading a book on fire.

The July night was smothering the avenue with its steamy kisses. The purse-snatchers were already cracking their knuckles in doorways while we strolled arm in arm, stopping only to grab each other by the crotch and talk breathlessly of Calabrian sausages and Romano cheese.

The entire play consists of monologues and asides by a dozen actors who are on the stage all at the same time. They pay no attention to each other even though their speeches are inordinately passionate. They rant, snort, foam at the mouth for almost three hours. One of the actresses is stark naked, one of the actors is dressed as a general, another has a rope around his neck, there's an old woman scrubbing the floor under his feet and a dog who walks on his hind legs.

And in the background, canned laughter by a Chinese audience.

Melancholy Senorita Miranda waiting for me on her veranda. "I'm an obituary writer on a holiday," I said to her.

"When the entire world was covered with ladybugs," she sighed, "and we made love on the ceiling."

Dog races in dreams: I occasionally saw a man on all fours trying to keep up.

Compose yourself, my friend, these must be the madonnas of Hieronymus Bosch riding the A-train after midnight.

"Do I look like Nostradamus?" he says to his reflection in the window of a store selling fire-damaged furniture.

I ask about heaven and hell. X ponders with eyes closed. Y continues to gorge himself on bread and butter, and Z studies the ceiling as if it were his navel.

The plot thickens. Nadine barges in wearing a new black bikini. She wants to know what we think of it? We think she ought to turn around, once, twice . . . except for Z, who continues to regard the ceiling with a beseeching air.

Early one morning a young woman in black dress and high heels fishing from a bridge on the way to Portsmouth.

I only have my king left on the chessboard, and he is cornered, while my invisible opponent has all his figures still in play.

"It must be one of the World's Great Masters I'm playing?" I shout.

"It's your fate, dummy," the naked woman in bed says.

"In that case," I tell her, "come over and sit in my lap. After we get nice and snug, I'll think of some clever move."

I shared the solitude of my childhood with a black cat. I sat on the window for hours on end watching the empty street while she sat on the bed washing herself. When night fell, I lay on the bed and she watched the street.

Round about midnight, the phone in the booth on the corner would ring a long time, but no one ever came to answer it. After that the cat's tail would flicker a long time until it put me to sleep.

On rainy days, I played chess with the cat, who pretended to doze. Once, when my mother turned on the table lamp, the silhouettes of the few remaining chess figures could be seen clearly on the wall. I was afraid to move. I didn't even take a breath.

When I finally did, the cat had vanished, taking the chess set with it and leaving me as I was in the same mean little room with its one window and its view of the empty street.

Child of the night, hold a mirror in your hand like an open book and call out the names of your father and mother, first name, last name, as they were called out long ago on their first day of school. When your neighbor bangs on the wall, shout even louder, shriek!

while watching them stare back at you out of the dim mirror.

A cold, clear night, good for radio reception of distant stations, some peddler of the divine from across the continent.

I remember soaping the crotch of a certain Miss L. in the sea at dusk, while she soaped mine. The water was cold, but we were burning. Our kisses made the sun take its time setting.

Eye to eye with the fly on the wall. "My luck quit for a while," he says. "I see yours is holding still."

I ran into the poet Mark Strand on the street. He immediately challenged me by drinking a glass of red wine while standing on his head. I was astonished! He didn't even spill a drop. It was the same bottle that the great French poet, Charles Baudelaire, never got to finish because his mistress crawled into the room on all fours looking for one of her hairpins.

"Is this what is called magic realism?" I asked him. Years ago this same Strand translated a Quechua poem about a man raising a fly with wings of gold in a green bottle, and now look at him!

In B. everyone's first name seems to be Homer. The local pastime is slapping mosquitoes on each other's foreheads. The blind photographer sits on the porch snapping pictures of his barking dog. The mortician's young wife sings like a bird in a cage when she hangs her laundry.

"I suffer from a rare variety of bad luck which has an occasional unexpected happiness in store for me," the beggar said to me.

My bad luck, on the other hand, loves to entertain me with its practical jokes. I had just learned how to say, "More cookies Mom," when a German bomb fell on the house across the street. No sooner had I learned how to ride a bike than luck decorated the trees along country roads with men hanging from their branches. And so it went.

You're fifty-eight years old today. It's Sunday, so school is out except for a couple necking in the front of the classroom. Their tongues, which go around each other, are savage with ink.

You close your eyes to make sure. You open them again to verify the wiped blackboard, the wall clock for some reason cadaverous to read, while the two of them exit, the girl on crutches, dragging her foot behind.

It's raining and the sidewalks are slippery. He walks quickly with a schoolbook over his head, the one on crutches, falling behind with each step, shouts to him to not worry, to hurry home . . .

A hearse with a coffin stopped by the movie house so that its driver could shoot the breeze with the ticket seller. The movie showing was called *Diabolique*.

A complete stranger came to me one night on Forty-fourth Street and said I reminded him of his dead brother.

Every night I go down on my knees just to say this in your keyhole:

"Peddler of falsehoods, lover of death's latest gadgetry, murder's helper, instigator of lynching mobs, gourmet of other people's sufferings," etc., etc.

"Hey, fart catcher," he shouts from the inside! "Small-beer philosopher, king of bird shit working yourself into a fit, your kind was born only to be stepped on like roaches," etc., etc.

The infinite riches of an empty room. Silence makes visible what now appears to be the most interesting grain of dust in the whole world.

Miniature philosophers: the kind you keep in our pocket. "Are you Pico della Mirandola?" I said to the tip of a toothpick lying in the palm of my hand. "If so, make me think big thoughts on subjects the world regards as being of no consequence."

It's so quiet, I can hear that something which is always eavesdropping on my life make a slight noise, the kind a letter makes sliding into a mailbox that has no name.

Better knock on wood, I thought, making the stopped clock on the dining-room table jump with the three loud knocks.

My philosophical views were shrouded in obscurity. My only true disciple was a black cat who kept crossing the street in front of me, making me stop dead in my tracks.

Every day a nervous fit. "Why do you keep staring at me like a professor of algebra?" I asked my conscience. "Go back to your seat, dummy," he ordered me, while I kept mulling over new ways to insult him.

"Why is it that we never laugh when we tickle ourselves?" I shouted from the last row. How come some girl only has to wag her little finger at us and we plop down cackling on the floor, begging her for mercy?

"Think about it, too," I said to the puss coming over to rub herself against my leg on the street.

V

ROUND MIDNIGHT

I like the black keys better.
I like lights turned down low.
I like women who drink alone
While I hunch over the piano
Looking for the pretty notes.

In my dream, I took a taxi to China to see the Great Wall.

There's a picture of me when I was five years old. I'm grinning while some unknown grown-up's hands cover my eyes.

The hope is that the poem turns out to be better than the poet.

We live in nameless present convinced if we give things names we will know where we are.

Tate: "It's a tragic story, but that's what's so funny."

Consciousness: The light bulb we are handed at birth.

As far as I'm concerned, it is not a contradiction to say that God both does and does not exist.

Paintings and photographs on the walls of a bar in Berlin. One is a photo of a woman giving a man a blow job. Seated at the table directly underneath, two elderly ladies chatting over their drinks.

The President says: "Let's drop bombs on some country until they start loving us."

A brightly-lit cash machine in a slum.

Looking for a cure for a dead horse in Iraq, politicians, generals, newspaper columnists all offering their miracle cures.

Even prisoners look back and say: "Ah that was a great day. We were all out in the yard. The sun was shining, I was sunbathing, and I said to myself, 'God, I feel so good!'"

It's not like people anywhere are jumping around and shouting, "Oh my God! Another poet! Aren't we lucky?"

If you asked my grandmother any question about the past, she would reply this way: "Of course, I remember the day the War started. The night before your grand-father said to me, 'Mitzo, it's been a long time since we had veal chops. Why don't we have some veal chops tomorrow?' So I'm thinking, 'Well, let's see, veal chops, I used to go to so-and-so for them, but last time the veal was so tough, I'd better go to see another butcher tomorrow morning.'"

With its bloodshot eye, the window searches the evening sky.

Kenneth Patchen: "like a mirror held to music."

Back numbers of girlie magazines at the dump chastely covered with new snow.

A runny, red nose on the subway, dripping into Kierkegaard's *Fear and Trembling*.

Grim Reaper is now my chaperon.

A pimpmobile parked under a palm tree outside a desert casino.

A man on all fours chasing a little dog in the park.

Don't snore so loud, my love.

Drinking vintage Chateau Margot from a Hellmann's mayonnaise jar in Rosa's kitchen.

I used to have a few imaginary friends. We used to lie in bed at night and tell each other about our travels to Africa.

Miss Brown, long-legged like a chicken coop.

A window thick with exotic plants. They live in a jungle, I think. They have a tiger for a sofa; use an alligator for a coffee table. Their children run around like monkeys. When father opens his mouth to speak, the air fills with fireflies. When his wife lifts her skirt to show him her purple stockings, the parrots shriek.

Those smiling faces one saw at lynchings a hundred years ago are back among us and are still smiling.

That must have been Ivan the Terrible I saw playing the accordion on the street corner in Berlin.

A book of love poems that will put Viagra out of business.

In the park yesterday: A body-builder on roller skates, young mother pushing a pram, Chinese waiter whose shoes pinch, lovers sharing a slice of pizza, old lady who used to date Dracula, teenage Jesus and his friend Elvis, a cutie in short skirt and combat boots, the lone bongo-player with wrap-around shades.

A moonbeam in a letter office. A postcard faded beyond recognition with someone like Persephone on the postage stamp.

As for my insomnia, it was like being led to the gallows each night and asked to say a few words.

My only friends, my playmates: the little thoughts in my head.

This morning, rummaging through a drawer, I found one of my baby photographs. The little fatso looked happy. With the few dark hairs on his head carefully combed. One could see he was itching for some lady to pick him up and show him a good time.

Faulkner somewhere defines poetry as the whole history of the human heart on a head of a pin.

Where words fail and amazement takes over: the silence of the night lit up with stars. To speak of God at this moment would be a blasphemy.

The secret ambition of any literary work is to make gods and devils take notice.

She was like a snake-charmer in a thrift shop mink coat.

Clever flies,
all abuzz
'round the president's
brand new turd.

Desdemona, Juliet, Ophelia, Lady Macbeth and me painting the town red.

Gods have poetry to thank for finding themselves in heaven.

Was that the gravedigger I saw you run from? He left his muddy fingerprints on your white dress while we stood around holding our wine glasses and laughing. Then, you both vanished and so did we, making our way in silence up to the dark house on the hill.

They were cutting someone's throat in a field across the road. "Can I go and watch?" I asked my mother, God forgive me.

A poem is like a bank robbery: The idea is to get in, get their attention, get the money and get out.

Don't you hear me bang my head against your wall? Of course, you do, you cowards! So how come you don't answer me? Bang your head on your side of the wall and keep me company.

The horrors of our time will make us nostalgic for those of the past.

Pere Simic's advice: Treat yourself, son. Drink a good bottle of cheap wine.

What an outrage! This very moment gone forever.

Illegible scribble, tangle of unfinished thoughts, tell me, is this God's thumbprint I'm lost in? Or some demon's late night coffee dregs?

On a night like this, one ought to serve hot soup to oxen. In the village church, the saints have forgotten all about God and are watching the snow fall.

The orchestra conductor has lifted his baton. Since then, it's been hours. Once in a while there's a cough, a sneeze and more discreetly the sound of someone snoring.

In the shadow of murderers at work, we kicked a ball made of rags. My friends, my old playmates, we didn't see the gallows, only crows storming the sky as we ran home to our mothers.

He could read the mind of a lit match as it entered a dark room.

The wind is bored with the trees; the sea is bored with the rocks; the children are bored in school; their parents are bored in church.

"I had a bellyful of your love," a man shouts into a cell phone as he passes me on the street.

The devil is always scribbling something. Neighbors try

to peek over his shoulders, flies, and even God himself. When people ask him what he's writing, he tells them *nothing*. And yet, they say, his pockets are full of worn-out erasers and pencil stubs.

And as for you, grandma, what have you done with the truth? The one you held once by the kitchen sink, like a drop of water in the palm of your hand.

We are blind beggars with arms linked making our slow way on a crowded avenue. I play the guitar, and you rattle a tin cup as we sing in high-pitched voices, *Dark is the night, cold is the ground, Oh Lord, please remember me.*

And there you were, father, with your white hair, white shirt, white pants, all alone in mid-day heat on a street of white buildings with no one else in view, except someone lost like me, too spooked to ask for directions.

Pious hypocrites, windbags for sale, firebugs with global ambitions, inventors of scapegoats, money-grabbing clergymen, thieves of poor children's lunches, cowards penning war editorials, millions of soulless bastards, let this little old lady and her old dog cross the street.

At the dive where Orion is the bartender, the usual crowd of insomniacs munching salty zeroes from a peanut bowl while watching some girl do the bump and grind to the silence of the infinite.

What can the white screen be thinking as the movie ends?

Here's an idea. I'll borrow money and hire a pretty young actress to stand in my room shouting night and day, "Free me from this hell!"

People tell about a blind man who rolled dice on the sidewalk and paid the neighborhood children a quarter to read the numbers for him.

The tuba in the pawnshop window misses the marching band and the long-legged majorette twirling her baton out in front as she steps down the avenue. She may turn up some day yet, with a radio under her arm or a double-barrel shotgun.

My friends, my playmates, the thoughts in my head, and you dear ghosts, everything outside this moment is a lie.

In times of lies and violence, the dire necessity of going mad, a question of honor I do not expect to be met with understanding.

Long ago, misfortune made me her dreamboat, befuddling my wits with questions. What makes me deserve all this? My playing hard-to-get is no use.

One mad idea after another let loose upon the world as if they were soap bubbles and we small children running after them.

The lizard stares unblinking at the rocks as if they were a row of TV sets all tuned to the evening news.

My white hair in a store window like a wind-thumbed Bible some street preacher tossed in the air.

In bad luck's auction room you always draw a huge crowd of bidders.

Of course, God is equally clueless why we are here. Henrietta doesn't believe me. She nods to the clergyman on his way to make pastoral visits in the neighborhood. Does this make me sore? You bet it does.

As for S., he now found himself face to face with things, which, if they consented to be understood, did so with great reluctance. Like growing old.

Insomnia. A lifelong dereliction of duty. A form of rebellion against the whole of eternity. A spit in its eye, as it were.

Gluttons of other people's sufferings, the time of fabulous feasts is coming.

An Assyrian stele in a museum depicting prisoners of war in a file whipped by their guards as they march. They all have identical beards, identical expressions and clothing and are completely interchangeable.

Finally a just war; all the innocents killed in it can regard themselves as lucky.

This must be the window where Edgar Allan Poe used to peek out on dark and stormy nights.

He read the papers with mounting satisfaction that everything is going to hell, just as he predicted.

The truth is, we are nearer to heaven each time we lie down. If you don't believe look at the cat rolled over with his feet in the air. A sunny morning after the last night's storm is an invitation to paradise, so we leapt out of bed to dress in a hurry, only to linger kissing and edge our way toward the bed again, astonished to find the ceiling over our heads, and not the blue sky.

Douce now, bare-assed Venus,
The fleas are awake.
The monster is in bed.
A naked light bulb over his head.

Naked women in the museum give the impression of liking to be looked at.

One-eyed cat in a fish store window.

Vacancy sign hung out on a windy evening to screech and keep us awake.

Who was my first ancestor to whistle in the dark?

The horror of a line that has just realized it's been drawn toward infinity.

Labyrinthine cities of the mind where I'm always getting lost.

Olga the Bearded Lady was a daughter of a Hungarian general, half-sister of a French Duke, native of Paris,

Moscow, Shanghai and New Jersey. This is nearly the story of my mother.

My father knew the network of passages connecting the Grand Central to the surrounding office buildings and hotels. He knew every cigar stand, public bathroom, shoe shine parlor and bar where he was greeted with cheer because he always left huge tips.

The simpler the object the vaster the dream.

The attentive eye begins to hear.

Everything, of course, is a mirror if you look at it long enough.

Bartleby giving up his work to stare at the blank wall outside his window always made sense to me.

The very pretty and now silent music box.

The thought that some nation out there in the world is not getting its just deserts always sends our armchair bombardiers into deep funk.

The porcupine crossing the busy highway with its quills erect.

Today's Special: Baby lamb snatched from its mother, quickly skinned and slowly roasted.

If you bathe a cat, it will rain. If you bathe two cats—what happens then?

A broken refrigerator in the yard next to the plaster statues of the Virgin.

Descartes, I hear, did his best philosophizing by lazing in bed past noon. Not me! I'm on the way to the dump, tooting my horn and waving to the neighbors.

The mutt under the table eavesdrops on the love letter I'm writing and sighs.

The moon tonight is like the ass of a young bride squatting down to pee.

I was a fly on the ceiling in the house of arachnids, watching and listening as they sipped the red tea of sunset in the parlor.

Memphis Minnie singing: Hoodoo lady, you who turn water into wine, I wonder where you been hiding yourself all this time.

Grandmother dressing a little girl in white in a city to be bombed that day.

Playing house with you in a matchbox—that would be something!

A rolled newspaper with the president's picture on the front page with which she goes searching for flies to kill.

The only concept of the state Republicans understand is the one in which the rich get richer by stealing from everyone else.

Tarpaper shanty with plastic over its windows and Bush/ Cheney election sign in front.

It's so quiet, one can hear the sound of the waves Homer heard on the Aegean.

My insomnia: An iceberg split from Infinity's Pole.

The secret room was full of toys of dead children.

O Tristia, let's get into bed and love each other till the bedsprings start to cry.

Three drunks on piano, guitar and saxophone playing "My Funny Valentine" in a corner saloon.

When aspiring mass murderers are so much admired among us . . . Clearly, the nation feels strongly that there hasn't been enough misery in the world, and that much more is wanted, so, of course, more is what we are going to get.

This crow nodding his head and putting down his foot with all due precaution, must've been a professor of philosophy in previous life who despite changed circumstances continues to turn things over in his mind, opening his beak wide as if to address his adoring students, and seeing nothing but a few fat snowflakes, resumes his stroll watched closely by another crow sitting glumly in a tree.

Artaud: "The hideous imprisonment of poetry in language." Damn right! No! Damn wrong.

Nature gets bored too. That's why it likes to see earth-quakes, hurricanes, erupting volcanoes and old folk dying.

A clock that goes to 13. Was it in one of Philip Guston's paintings that I saw it?

"Simic," he said, "Why don't you dye your hair green like Baudelaire?"

That woman's bare ass is more attractive to me than paradise.

And then, one suspects, there were a few here and there who actually died laughing.

Cold, windy autumn night. A homeless woman on the corner talking to God, and he, as usual, having nothing to say.

It's like rain in a silent movie, or like a ship on the bottom of the sea, or like a house of mirrors at closing time, or like the grave of the world-famous ventriloquist, or like the face of the bride as she sits down to pee after a night of love, or like a shirt drying on the line with no house near . . . Anyway, you get the idea.

I don't believe in God, but I'm afraid of opening an umbrella inside the house.

Another century in which anyone who thought deeply found himself alone and speechless.

Anywhere conformity is an ideal, poetry is not welcome.

There are no keyholes left anywhere for old men like me to peep through, save on a gate to the cemetery with not much to see beyond but rows of well-tended graves. Wherever they're shedding their clothes, they are not doing it here. There are a few fresh flags in view, a robin with a straw in its beak but no lace panties draped over tombstones.

According to Cioran, silence is as old as being, perhaps even older. He means the silence before there was time. This is the only God I believe in.

The rooster wears a bishop's miter with the hens trailing after him nodding their heads and clucking after his early morning homily. The black and white mutt has found religion, too, barking at a cat in a tree, who sits watching the leaves fly.

Peck sparrows and you pigeons. Whoever is shaking the tablecloth with breadcrumbs of good and evil appears to be busy somewhere else today.

Acknowledgments

Selections from this book first appeared in *Wonderful Words, Silent Truth*, University of Michigan Press, Ann Arbor, 1990. © 1990 by Charles Simic. Reprinted with the kind permission of the publisher.

Thanks to *The Ohio Review*, *The London Review of Books*, and *Field*, which first published other selections.

Ausable Press is especially grateful to Varujan Boghosian, Kathryn and David Heleniak, Christina Lau and Lori Bookstein Fine Art for their extraordinary efforts in arranging for the use of the cover art. Thanks also to Sheila Schwartz of the Saul Steinberg Foundation and Karen Nangle of the Beinecke Rare Book and Manuscript Library.

Ausable Press would like to thank

The New York State Council on the Arts

The National Endowment for the Arts

The New York Community Trust

for their generous support.